S0-AZF-778

Meals Around the World

Meals in Mexico

by Cari Meister

Bullfrog
Books

Ideas for Parents and Teachers

Bullfrog Books let children practice reading informational text at the earliest reading levels. Repetition, familiar words, and photo labels support early readers.

Before Reading

- Discuss the cover photo. What does it tell them?

- Look at the picture glossary together. Read and discuss the words.

Read the Book

- "Walk" through the book and look at the photos. Let the child ask questions. Point out the photo labels.

- Read the book to the child, or have him or her read independently.

After Reading

- Prompt the child to think more. Ask: Have you ever eaten Mexican food? Were the flavors new to you? What did you like best?

Bullfrog Books are published by Jump!
5357 Penn Avenue South
Minneapolis, MN 55419
www.jumplibrary.com

Library of Congress Cataloging-in-Publication Data

Names: Meister, Cari, author.
Title: Meals in Mexico / by Cari Meister.
Description: Minneapolis, MN: Jump!, Inc., [2016]
© 2017 | Series: Meals around the world
"Bullfrog Books are published by Jump!."
Audience: Ages 5–8. | Audience: K to grade 3.
Includes recipes. | Includes index.
Identifiers: LCCN 2016011661 (print)
LCCN 2016013041 (ebook)
ISBN 9781620313749 (hardcover: alk. paper)
ISBN 9781620314920 (pbk.)
ISBN 9781624964213 (ebook)
Subjects: LCSH: Cooking, Mexican—Juvenile literature. | Food habits—Mexico—Juvenile literature.
Classification: LCC TX716.M4 M4275 2016 (print)
LCC TX716.M4 (ebook) | DDC 641.5972—dc23
LC record available at http://lccn.loc.gov/2016011661

Editor: Jenny Fretland VanVoorst
Series Designer: Ellen Huber
Book Designer: Leah Sanders
Photo Researcher: Leah Sanders

Photo Credits: All photos by Shutterstock except: Corbis, 6–7; Getty, 5, 12, 20–21; iStock, 4, 8–9, 18–19; Thinkstock, 23br.

Printed in the United States of America at Corporate Graphics in North Mankato, Minnesota.

Table of Contents

Ring! Ring!

Ring! Ring!

It is snack time at school.

Leo has papas.

Rosa eats a melon.

Zoe runs to the vendor.
She buys a churro.
It is warm. It is sweet.
We go back to class.

churro

Ring! Ring!
Now school is out.
We go home to eat.

In Mexico, the big meal is in late afternoon.

We have soup first.

We drink jamaica.

jamaica

We have tortillas and beans.

tortillas

beans

12

We have meat and rice.

We eat it with salsa.

It is spicy.

salsa

It is a big day.
Marta makes
special food.

She makes pozole.

It is a corn stew.

Lita makes tamales.

There is flan for dessert.
Yum!

Make Flan!

**Make this yummy dessert from Mexico!
Be sure to get an adult to help.**

Ingredients:

- 1½ cup sugar
- 6 eggs
- 2 13-ounce cans evaporated milk
- 1 14-ounce can sweetened condensed milk
- 1½ teaspoon vanilla

Directions:

❶ Preheat oven to 325 degrees.
❷ Put 1 cup sugar in pan on medium heat.
❸ Stir until sugar browns and becomes caramel.
❹ Pour caramel in round baking pan.
❺ In a separate bowl, whisk the eggs.
❻ Mix in the cans of both milks.
❼ Add ½ cup of sugar and the vanilla.
❽ Blend until smooth.
❾ Pour custard mixture into the caramel pan.
❿ Put pan into large glass baking dish and fill with 2 inches of hot water.
⓫ Bake for 45 minutes.
⓬ Let cool in the refrigerator for an hour.
⓭ To serve, turn the pan over.

Picture Glossary

churro
A long, fried pastry with cinnamon and sugar.

salsa
A spicy sauce of tomatoes, onions, and hot peppers.

jamaica
A cold, tart tea made from hibiscus flowers.

tamales
Spiced meat in corn dough that is wrapped in corn husks or banana leaves.

papas
Potatoes or potato chips.

vendor
A person who sells things.

Index

To Learn More

Learning more is as easy as 1, 2, 3.

1) Go to www.factsurfer.com

2) Enter "mealsinMexico" into the search box.

3) Click the "Surf" button to see a list of websites.

With factsurfer.com, finding more information is just a click away.